BOOKS BY **ROBERT E. DALEY**

A Case for "Threes"
A Simple Plan . . . of Immense Complexity
Armour, Weapons, And Warfare
from Everlasting to Everlasting
Killer Sex
Life or Death, Heaven or Hell, You Choose!
Raptures and Resurrections
Short Tales
So . . . What Happens to the Package?
Study and Interpretation of The Scriptures Made Simple
Surviving Destruction as A Human Being
The Gospel of John
The Gospel of John (Red Edition)
The League of The Immortals
The New Testament - Pauline Revelation
The New Testament - Pauline Revelation Companion
"The World That Then Was . . ." & The Genesis That Now Is
What Color Are You?
What Makes A Christian Flaky?
What Really Happened to Judas Iscariot?
Who YOU Are in Christ . . . RIGHT NOW!

The Enhancement Series

    #1 Book of Ecclesiastes
    #2 Book of Daniel
    #3 Book of Romans
    #4 Book of Galatians
    #5 Book of Hebrews

The Deeper Things of God Series

    #1 The Personage of God
    #2 The Personage of Man
    #3 The Personage of Christ

The Enhancement Series • Book Four

THE NEW TESTAMENT

BOOK OF GALATIANS

EXPLOSIVELY ENHANCED

This is an independent work, utilizing the
King James Translation of the Bible, with author
enhancement for clarity and presentation of intended thought.

Robert E. Daley

The Larry Czerwonka Company, LLC
Hilo, Hawai'i

First Edition — November 2014

This book is set in 14-point Garamond

Published by: The Larry Czerwonka Company,
LLChttp://thelarryczerwonkacompany.com

Printed in the United States of America

ISBN: 0692330151
ISBN-13: 978-0692330159

All scriptures used in this work are taken from the
King James Version of the Scriptures.

Introduction

The sole purpose for enhancement is for simple clarity.

In this work, the King James Translation of the Bible is unchanged within its textual record.Punctuation and translator added words may be altered, but the singular purpose behind that, is for clear understanding by the reader.

Since the book is a doctrinal thesis concerning adherence to the Law of Moses, verses the grace of God revealed within the finished work of Christ Jesus on the cross, it is important that the student of the word of God have a clear cognizance of spiritual truth.Drastic spiritual changes have occurred upon the resurrection of the New Creation Lord, Jesus Christ of Nazareth.Changes that are largely unknown, or at the very least, unrecognized by modern day Christianity may be clearly seen here.

This work presents the reality that there are now three separate "types" of Human-Beings in existence, that are now living here on this planet, Earth.These three "types" ofHuman-Beings are:the **Gentile**, the **Jew**, and the **New Creation**.

Failure to understand this reality, will most assuredly lead to spiritual confusion, and religious insistence.

Division will be the end result, just as it was within the Scriptural letter that was addressed to the Corinthian church.

This author desires that all Christians become fully aware of who they are now in Christ, after having asked Jesus of Nazareth to "save" them, and then to direct them by his Holy Spirit, in their continual walk with God.

THE BOOK OF
GALATIANS

CHAPTER 1

1.   Paul *of Tarsus,* an apostle *of God,* (not *appointed* of men, neither *approved* by *any* man, but *called and commissioned* by *the New Creation Lord,* **Jesus Christ** *of Nazareth,* and *by* **God the Father, who raised him** *up again* **from the dead;)**

2.   **And all** *of* **the brethren which are** *currently* **with me;** *Greetings* **unto the churches of Galatia:**

3.   *I pray that the* **grace** *of God* ***be*** *ministered un***to you, and** *the* **peace** *that passes all understanding,* **from God the Father, and** ***from*** **our** *New Creation* **Lord Jesus Christ.**

4.   **Who** *personally* **gave himself,** *in a selfless sacrifice* **for our sins, that he might deliver us from this present evil world,** *should we choose to receive and accept it,* **according to the will of God and our father:**

5.   **To whom** ***be*** **glory** *and honour* **for ever and ever. Amen.**

6.   **I marvel** *indeed* **that ye are so soon removed from him that** *originally* **called you into the grace of Christ, unto another gospel.**

7.   Which is *really* not another; but *sadly* there be some *individuals* that trouble you, and would *desire to* pervert the gospel of Christ.

8.   But though we *ourselves*, or *even* an angel from heaven, preach any other gospel unto you than that which we have *originally* preached unto you, let him be accursed.

9.   As we *have* said before, so say I now *personally* again, If any *man* preach *or promote* any other gospel unto you than that *which* ye have *already* received *from us*, let him be accursed.

10.   For do I now *endeavor to* persuade men, or *to serve* God? Or do I seek to *be* pleas*ing unto* men? For if I yet pleased men, I should not be *worthy to be* the servant of Christ.

11.   But I certify *unto* you, *my* brethren, that the gospel which was preached of me is not after man.

12.   For I neither received it of *any* man, neither was I taught *it*, but by the *direct* revelation of Jesus Christ.

13.   For ye have heard of my *expressed* conversation in time past in the Jew's religion *of Judaism*, how that beyond measure I persecuted the church of God, and wasted it.

14.   And *I indeed* profited in the Jews' religion above many *of* my equals *with*in mine *own* nation,

being more exceedingly zealous of the *religious* traditions of my fathers.

15. But when, *in the course of time,* it pleased God, who separated me from my mother's womb, and *personally* called *me* by his grace,

16. To *wondrously* reveal *the miracle of* his Son in me, that I might preach him among the heathen *barbarian, pagan, unbelieving Gentiles*: immediately I conferred not with flesh and blood.

17. Neither went I up to Jerusalem to them which were *ordained as* apostles before me; but I went *immediately* into Arabia *where I was instructed by Christ Jesus himself concerning the reality of that which had occurred at the time of his resurrection,* and *upon my initial instruction conclusion,* I returned again unto Damascus.

18. Then after three years *of ministering the revelation word of God,* I went up to Jerusalem, *because of death threats,* to see *and to speak to* Peter, and *I* abode with him *for* fifteen days.

19. But *any* other of the apostles saw I none, save *for* James the Lord's *half*-brother.

20. Now the things which I *now* write unto you *my brethren,* behold, before God, I lie not.

21. Afterward, *because of further death threats,* I came *back* into the regions of Syria and Cilicia *from which I had originally come.*

22. And *I* was unknown by face unto the *rest of the* churches of Judea which were in Christ.

23. But they had heard only, That he which *has severely* persecuted us in *the* times *since* past, now preacheth the *very* faith which once he destroyed.

24. And they glorified God *for what he had done* in me.

CHAPTER 2

1. Then fourteen years after I *had gone back home, to the city of Tarsus in the region of Cilicia, Barnabas came and sought me out, and brought me back into fellowship once again, within the church in the city of Antioch. (Acts 11:22-26) And, at a point in time,* I went up again *un*to *the city of* Jerusalem with Barnabas, and *I* took Titus with *me* also.

2. And I went up by revelation *approval of the Lord Jesus*, and communicated unto them *within Jerusalem*, that *revelation* gospel which I preach among the *heathen, barbarian, pagan, unbelieving* Gentiles. But *first* privately, to them which were of reputation *within the church*, lest by any means I should run, or *rather* had run, in vain.

3. But neither *was* Titus *without assault*, who was *a ministering partner* with me. *And* being *from* a *Gentile* Greek *background*, he was compelled to be circumcised *according to the Law of Moses*.

4.   And that *occurred* because of false brethren unawares brought in*to the fellowship of the New Creation believers,* who came in privily *at their own discretion,* to spy out our *new found* liberty which we have in *the finished resurrection work* of **Christ Jesus.** *And their attempt, was* that they might bring us into *the* bondage *of the requirements of the Law of Moses once again.*

5.   To whom we gave *any* place by subjection *unto their demands?* **No! Not** *even* **for an hour,** that the *revelation* truth of the gospel might *be able to* continue with you.

6.   But of these *leaders in Jerusalem,* who seemed to be somewhat, (whatsoever they were, it maketh no matter to me: God accepteth no man's person.) For they who seemed *to be somewhat* in conference, added nothing to me.

7.   But contrariwise, when they *all* saw that the gospel *ministration* of the uncircumcision was *firmly* committed unto me, as **the gospel** *ministration* of the circumcision *was committed* unto **Peter;**

8.   (For he that wrought effectually in Peter to the apostleship of the circumcision, the same was *just as* mighty in me toward the **Gentiles)**

9.   And when James, *and* Cephas, and John, who seemed to be *the leading* pillars *of the church,* perceived *of* the grace that was given unto me *by the living God,* they gave *un*to me and Barnabas the

right hands of fellowship; that we *indeed **should go*** unto the heathen, and they *should go* unto the circumcision.

10.   Only ***they would*** *desire,* that we should *be mindful to* remember the *financially* poor *saints wherever we went;* the same which I also was forward to do.

11.   But *at the time* when Peter was come to Antioch *to visit the church,* I withstood him to the face, because he was to be blamed.

12.   For before that certain *Judaizers* came from James, he did eat *his meals* with the Gentiles. But when they were come *into the fellowship,* he withdrew and separated himself *in line with the Law of Moses,* fearing them which were of the circumcision.

13.   And the other *newly converted* Jews dissembled *and withdrew themselves* likewise with him. Insomuch that *even* Barnabas also was carried away with their dissimulation.

14.   But when I saw that they walked not uprightly according to the *revelation* truth of the gospel, I said unto Peter before ***them all,*** If thou, being a *New Creation* Jew, livest after the manner of *the newly converted New Creation* Gentiles, and not as do the *pre-conversion* Jews, why *would you want to* compellest thou the *newly converted New Creation* Gentiles to live as do the *pre-conversion* Jews?

15. We *who are* *originally* **Jews by nature, and not** *originally known of as* **sinners,** *like as* **of the** *pre-conversion* **Gentiles,**

16. *Now* **knowing that a man is not justified** *before God* **by the works of the Law** *of Moses*, **but by the** *very* **faith of Jesus Christ** *of Nazareth*, **even we have believed in Jesus Christ, that we might be justified** *before God* **by the faith of Christ** *Jesus alone*, **and not by the works of the** *Mosaic* **law. For by the works of the Law** *of Moses* **shall no flesh be** *able to be* **justified** *before God*.

17. **But if, while we seek to be justified** *before God* **by** *the faith of* **Christ** *Jesus alone*, **we ourselves also are found** *to be* **sinners** *according to the Law of Moses*, ***is*** **therefore Christ the minister of sin? God forbid!**

18. **For if I build again** *my trust in* **the things** *of the Law of Moses*, **which** *once* **I destroyed** *by placing my full trust in the finished work of Christ Jesus*, **I make myself a transgressor** *once again*.

19. **For I**, **through the** *new spiritual* **law** *of Life in Christ Jesus* *(Romans 8:2)*, **am dead to the Law** *of Moses*, **that I might live** *with my whole being* **unto God.**

20. **I am** *continually* **crucified with Christ, nevertheless I live. Yet** *it is* **not I, but Christ** *that* **liveth** *with*in **me. And the life which I now live in the flesh** *from day to day*, **I live by the faith of the Son of God** *alone*, **who loved me, and gave himself for me.**

21.   I do not frustrate the grace of *my* God *by trying to live according to the Law of Moses*. **For if** *the* **righteousness** *of my God* **comes** by the *keeping of the* **Law** *of Moses*, then **Christ** *Jesus* is *truly* **dead in vain.**

CHAPTER 3

1.   O *ye* **foolish Galatians, who hath** *seduced and* **bewitched you, that you should not obey the** *revelation* **truth** *that ye have heard?* **Before whose** *very* **eyes Jesus Christ** *of Nazareth* **has been** *presented, and* **evidently set forth,** *as being* **crucified among you?**
2.   **This only would I** *now* **learn of you;** *have you* **received ye the** *recreating, indwelling of the Holy* **Spirit** *of God,* **by the works of the Law** *of Moses,* **or by the hearing of faith?**
3.   **Are ye** *really* **so foolish** *that ye cannot see?* **Having begun** *your walk with the living God* **in the Spirit, are ye now made perfect by the** *works of the* **flesh?**
4.   **Have ye suffered so many things** *for naught, and* **in vain? If** *indeed,* ***it be*** **yet in vain.**
5.   **He therefore that ministereth** *un*to **you the** *Holy* **Spirit, and worketh miracles among you . . .** ***doeth he it*** **by the work***ing***s of the Law** *of Moses,* **or by the hearing of faith?**
6.   **Even as** *it is recorded within the Scriptures, that* **Abraham** *simply* **believed** *on* **God** *concerning the promise*

that God made to him, and it was accounted to him for righteousness.

7.   **Know ye therefore that** *today,* **they which are** *following the same path* **of faith** *in what God declares; that is, that the righteousness of God is found in the faith of what Christ Jesus alone has done,* **the same are the children of Abraham.**

8.   **And the Scripture, forseeing that God would justify the heathen,** *barbarian, pagan, unbelieving, Gentiles* **through** *the* **faith** *of Jesus Christ,* **preached before,** *in the promise that God had made,* **the gospel unto Abraham,** *saying,* **"In thee shall all nations be blessed."** *(Genesis 12:3)*

9.   **So then they which be of** *the* **faith** *of Jesus Christ,* **are blessed** *along* **with faithful Abraham.**

10.   **For,** *today,* **as many** *Jews, or Gentiles, or New Creatures* **as are of** *the belief that they are justified before God by* **the works of the Law** *of Moses,* **are** *still* **under the curse. For it is written, "Cursed** *is* **every one . . .** *Jew, Gentile, or New Creature* **. . . that continueth not in all things which are written** *with*in **the Book** *of Deuteronomy, which is part* **of the Law** *of Moses,* **to do them."** *(Deuteronomy 27:26)*

11.   **But that no man . . .** *Jew, or Gentile, or New Creature . . .* **is justified by the** *keeping of the Jewish Sabbath of commandment, or by the keeping of the Ten Commandments, or by the compelled celebrating of the Feasts of the Lord, or by the*

necessity of Circumcision, or by the keeping of the celebrations of the New Moons, or by the adhering to of any of the eating regulations of the Book of Leviticus, or by anything else that is incorporated with the **Law** *of Moses* **in the sight of God,** *it is* **evident. For,** *those individuals that are* **the just***ified because of the work of Jesus Christ* **shall live** *their life from day to day* **by** *the* **faith** *of Jesus Christ.* (Habakkuk 2:4)

12. **And the Law** *of Moses, and all of the works contained therein,* **is not of faith. But, the man that** *chooseth to* **doeth them, shall** *be compelled by the very Law of Moses, to* **live in them,** *but shall in no wise be justified before God by the things which he doeth.*

13. *Jesus* **Christ hath redeemed us from the curse of the Law** *of Moses***, being made a curse for us. For it is written, "Cursed** *is* **every one that hangeth on a tree."** (Deuteronomy 21:23)

14. **That the blessing of Abraham might come** *up***on the** *heathen, barbarian, pagan, unbelieving,* **Gentiles** *as well,* **through Jesus Christ.** *And* **that we** *all* **might receive the promise of the** *indwelling of the Holy* **Spirit through faith.**

15. **Brethren, I speak after the manner of men;** *Even* **though** *it be* **but a man's covenant, yet** *if it be* **ratified** *and* **confirmed,** *then* **no man** *may subtract from and* **disannulleth, or addeth** *anything* **thereto.**

16. **Now to Abraham and his** *predestinated* **"seed"** **were the promises made. He saith not, and to**

seeds, as of many; but as of *only* one, "And to thy seed," which is Christ *Jesus*. *(Genesis 3:15 & 21:12)*

17.   And this I say, *that* the *Abrahamic* Covenant *promise*, that was confirmed before *in Genesis chapter fifteen* of God, in *the person of the Burning Lamp, which was* Christ; the *Mosaic* law *of the keeping of the Jewish Sabbath of Commandment, or the keeping of the Ten Commandments, or the celebration of the Feasts of the Lord, or the necessity of Circumcision, or the keeping of the celebrations of the New Moons, or the adhering to of any of the eating regulations of the Book of Leviticus, or by adhering to anything else that is incorporated within that law*, which was four hundred and thirty years after, cannot *cancel, subtract, or* disannul, that it should make the *Abrahamic Covenant* promise of none effect.

18.   For if the inheritance *of all of the things of God's creation* be of the Law *of Moses*, *it is* no more of promise. But God gave *it* to Abraham by promise.

19.   Wherefore then *serveth* the Law *of Moses with all of its different aspects? And what was the reason that it was given?* It was added *to the oracles of God for the benefit of the Jewish people only*, because of transgressions, *un*til the *predestinated "seed" named Jesus of Nazareth* should come, to whom the *original* promise was made. *And it was* ordained by angels in the hand of a mediator.

20.   Now a mediator is not a *mediator* of *only* one *person*, but God *even as Three Persons* is *only* one *God*.

21.   *Is* the Law *of Moses* then *contrary to, and* against, the promises of God? God forbid! For if there had been a *portion of the Mosaic* law given, which could have given *Everlasting, Eternal, spiritual* life, *then* verily righteousness *before God* should have been *obtainable* by the *Mosaic* law.

22.   But the Scripture hath concluded all *men, both Jew and Gentile,* under sin, that the *fulfilled* promise by *the* faith of Jesus Christ might be given to *all of* them that *only* believe, *both Jew and Gentile alike.*

23.   But before *the* faith *of Jesus Christ* came, we were kept under the Law *of Moses.* Shut up unto the faith *of Jesus Christ* which should afterwards be revealed.

24.   Wherefore the Law *of Moses* was our schoolmaster, *given by God to only the Jewish people,* **to bring us** unto Christ, that we might *ultimately* be justified *before God* by *the* faith *of Jesus Christ.*

25.   But after that *the* faith *of Jesus Christ* is come, we are no longer *in need of being* under a schoolmaster.

26.   For ye are all, *both Jew and Gentile alike, become* the *New Creation* children of God by faith in Christ Jesus.

27.   For as many of you as have been baptized into *the body of* Christ *through the New-Birth,* have put on Christ *and you are no longer the same.*

28.   There is, *in Christ,* neither **Jew** nor *Gentile* Greek *any more.* There is neither bond nor free. There is neither male nor female. For ye are all one *New Creation* in Christ Jesus.

29.   And if ye be *Jesus* Christ's, then are ye Abraham's *predestinated* "seed", and heirs *of the entire created Universe* according to the *God declared* promise, *that was made by God to Abraham.*

CHAPTER 4

1.   Now I say *unto you a spiritual truth*: *That* the heir *of all of the wealth,* as long as he is *believing and behaving like* a child, differeth nothing from a servant, *even* though he be *legally the* lord of all.

2.   But *the child* is under *assigned* tutors, and governors *of his affairs,* until the time *comes that has been* appointed of the father.

3.   Even so we, *concerning spiritual matters,* when we were *yet* children, were *still* in bondage under *the restraints of sin, and* the elements of the world.

4.   But when the fullness of the *prophetical* time was come, God *purposed, and* sent forth his Son, made of a woman *that he might be fully a Human Being,*

and made under the *restrictions and the requirements of the* Law *of Moses, that he might operate within the Abrahamic Covenant parameters.*

5.　　*And he came with the expressed purpose* to redeem them that were under the Law *of Moses, that is, the Covenant Jewish people of the Nation of Israel. And that through that redemption provision,* that we might receive the adoption *privilege* of sons.

6.　　And because ye are *now legitimate* sons, God hath sent forth the *earnest of his Holy* Spirit; *which is the Spirit* of his Son into your hearts, crying *out,* Abba, Father.

7.　　Wherefore thou art no more *simply* a *Covenant* servant *of the Most High God,* but a*n actual* son; and if a *real* son, then an heir of *all that* God *has made,* through *his Only Begotten Son,* Christ *Jesus.*

8.　　Howbeit then, when ye *were a pagan heathen, and* knew not *the living* God, ye did *worship* service unto them which by *the very fact of* nature *itself,* are no gods.

9.　　But now, after that ye have known God *because of the New-Birth,* or rather *that ye* are *now* known of God, how turn ye *back* again *un*to the weak and beggarly elements *of the Law of Moses.* Whereunto ye desire again to be in bondage *rather than to be free?*

10.　　Ye observe *the lawfully required* days, and months, and times, and years.

11.   I am afraid of you, lest I have bestowed upon you labour, *concerning spiritual reality and truth,* in vain.

12.   Brethren, I beseech you *once again,* *to* be as I *am*; for I *am* as ye *are*: ye have not injured me at all.

13.   Ye know how *that* through infirmity of the flesh, *in the things which I endured for the gospel's sake,* I preached the gospel unto you at the first.

14.   And my temptation, *of the care of the churches daily,* (II Corinthians 11:28) which was in my flesh ye despised not, nor rejected; but *rather* received me as an angel of God, *even* as *if I were* Christ Jesus.

15.   Where is then the *manifested* blessedness *that* ye *once* spake of? For I bear you record, that, if *it had been* *even* possible, *and needful,* ye would have plucked out your own eyes, and have given them to me.

16.   Am I therefore *now* become your enemy, because I tell you the truth *about spiritual realities*?

17.   *Concerning those deceitful Judaizers,* they zealously affect you, *but* not well. Yea, they would exclude you *from their fellowship,* *for fear* that ye might *adversely* affect them.

18.   But *it is* good to be zealously affected always in *a* good *thing,* and not only when I am present with you.

17

19.   My little children, of whom I travail in *the New*-Birth again, until Christ be *solidly* formed *within* you.

20.   I desire to be present with you *even* now, and to change my *tone of* voice; for I stand in doubt of you.

21.   Tell me, ye that desire *so much* to be under the Law *of Moses,* do ye not hear *what* the Law *of Moses itself says?*

22.   For it is written *within the Book of Genesis,* that Abraham had two sons. *The first son was named Ishmael, who was* the one *that was birthed* by a bondmaid *named Hagar, and* the other *son, was named Isaac, who was birthed* by a freewoman *named Sarah.*

23.   But he *who was* birthed of the bondwoman was born after the flesh*, when Abraham went in unto her, and she conceived.* But he *that was birthed* of the freewoman *was miraculously brought forth* by *a* promise*, at the time appointed.*

24.   Which things are an allegory *of spiritual truth.* For these *are the two incidents, which* are *representative of* the two *Blood* Covenants. The one *Covenant, with the active Law of Moses is* from the mount Sinai, *and is that* which gendereth *un*to bondage *even unto today,* which is *represented by* Agar. *(who is really named Hagar)*

25.   For this Agar is *symbolically* mount Sinai in Arabia, and answereth to *the city of* Jerusalem which

now is, and is in bondage *to the Law of Moses, along* with her children.

26.   But *the City of the New* **Jerusalem which is above is** *symbolically* **free, which is the mother of us all** *if we are Born-Again and have put our trust in the finished work of Christ Jesus upon the cross of Calvary.*

27.   For it is written, "Rejoice, *thou* barren that bearest not; break forth and cry, thou that travailest not: for the desolate hath many more children than she which hath an husband." *(Isaiah 54:1)*

28.   *So* now, we *New Creation* brethren, as Isaac was, are the children of *a* promise.

29.   But *even* as *back* then, *during the days of Abraham,* he that was born after the flesh, *and was carnally minded,* persecuted him *that, because of a promise,* **was born** after the Spirit. *And* even so *it is* now.

30.   Nevertheless what saith the scripture? "Cast out the bondwoman and her son. For the son of the bondwoman shall not be heir with the son of the freewoman." *(Genesis 21:10)*

31.   So then, *my* brethren, we are not *the natural* children of the bondwoman, but *we are New Creation children* of the free *woman, because of our New Birth in Christ Jesus.*

CHAPTER 5

1.　　Stand fast therefore in the liberty *that has been provided from the Law of Moses, because of Resurrection Realities,* wherewith Christ *Jesus* hath made us free. And be not entangled again with*in* the yoke of bondage *that comes from the necessity of keeping all of the aspects of the Law of Moses.*

2.　　Behold, I Paul say unto you, that if ye be*come* circumcised *because the Law of Moses demands it,* or *insist on worshipping on the Sabbath Day of commandment because the Law of Moses demands it, or attempt to keep the Ten Commandments because the Law of Moses demands it, or attempt to adhere to the eating regulations of the Book of Leviticus because the Law of Moses demands it, or attempt to please God by obeying what the Law of Moses demands, in any other aspect, then* Christ shall profit you nothing.

3.　　For I testify *once* again to every man that *believeth that he* is *compelled to become* circumcised, *or to obey any other aspect of the Law of Moses because that is what God himself demands;* that he is *then* a debtor to do the whole law, *leaving nothing unfulfilled.*

4.　　Christ *Jesus, and his sin-breaking, finished work upon the cross of Calvary,* is become of no effect *or value* unto you. Whosoever of you *that believeth that you* are justified by *any of* the *works of the* Law *of Moses;* ye are fallen from grace.

5. For we, *of the New Creation,* through the *help of the Holy* Spirit, wait for the hope of righteousness by faith.

6. For in Jesus Christ neither *Jewish* circumcision, *nor Sabbath Day attendance, nor Ten Commandment obedience, nor eating regulations, nor any other "Law" requirements,* availeth any thing *of benefit.* Nor *any of that which may be done by the* uncircumcision *individuals either;* but *only the exercise of* faith which worketh by love.

7. Ye did run well *at the first.* Who did hinder you that ye should not obey the *revelation* truth *of the gospel?*

8. This persuasion *cometh* not of him that calleth you, *that is, that this doctrine is not coming from God.*

9. *Do you not know, that* a little leaven leaveneth the whole lump?

10. *However,* I *still* have confidence in you through the Lord, that ye will *recognize the truth; and* be*come* none otherwise minded. But *know assuredly, that* he that troubleth you *with this false doctrine,* shall bear his judgment, whosoever he *may* be.

11. And I *myself,* brethren, if I yet *continue to* preach *"Law"* circumcision *obedience,* why do I yet suffer persecution *from those of the Jewish circumcision persuasion?* Then is the offence,*which is presented of* liberty, *through* the cross *of Christ Jesus,* ceased.

12.   I would *desire that* they were even cut off which *continue to* trouble you.

13.   For, brethren, ye have been called unto *the* liberty *that is found within the Resurrection Realities of the cross.* Only *use* not *that* liberty for an occasion to *go back to the demands of* the flesh *or the soul,* but by *the* love *of God,* serve one another.

14.   For all *of* the Law *of Moses* is *completely* fulfilled in one word, *even* in this; "Thou shalt love thy neighbor as thyself." *(Matthew 22:37-40)*

15.   But if ye *continue to* bite and devour one another *over doctrinal discrepancies,* take heed that ye be not *ultimately* consumed one of another.

16.   *This* I say then, Walk in the *leading of the newly,* Born-Again, recreated, Human spirit, and ye shall not fulfill the lust of the flesh.

17.   For the flesh *and the soul* lusteth against the *newly, Born-Again, recreated, Human* spirit, and the *newly, Born-Again, recreated, Human* spirit *contends* against the flesh. And these *two aspects of the redeemed Human Being* are contrary the one to the other: so that ye cannot *readily* do the things that ye would *spiritually want to do.*

18.   But if ye be led of the *newly, Born-Again, recreat-ed, Human* **spirit, ye are not under the** *compulsion mandates, or dictates, of the* **Law** *of Moses any more.*

19.   **Now the works of the flesh,** *and of the soul* **are manifest, which are** *these,* **adultery,** *which is inappropriate sexual activity by a married person, with someone outside of their marriage covenant,* **fornication,** *which is inappropriate sexual activity by individuals outside of a marriage covenant,* **uncleanness,** *which is whatever is opposite of purity, including sodomy, homosexuality, lesbianism, bestiality, and all other forms of inappropriate sexual perversion,* **lasciviousness,** *which is the promoting of, or partaking of, that which tends to produce lewd emotions, and anything that tends to foster lust, inappropriate sex, or sin,*

20.   **Idolatry,** *which includes image worship and anything on which affections are passionately set,* **witchcraft,** *which is sorcery and the practice of dealing with evil spirits, including magical incantations and the casting of spells and charms upon someone by means of drugs and potions of various kinds,* **ha-tred,** *which is bitter disdain, abhorrence, malice, and ill-will against anyone,* **variance,** *which is dissensions, discord, quarreling, debating, and disrupting,* **emulations,** *which are jealousies and striving to excel at the expense of another, including uncurbed rivalry in the areas of religion, business, society, and other fields of endeavor,* **wrath,** *which is turbulent passions, domestic and civil turmoils, rage, and determined and lasting anger,* **strife,** *which is disputations, janglings, and contention* *about words, or contesting for superiority or advantage, including strenuous endeavor to equal or pay back in like, the wrongs done to you,* **seditions,** *which is popular disorder in stirring up strife in religion, government, home, or any other place,* **heresies,** *which simply refers to a doctrinal view or belief at odds with the recognized and accepted tenets of a system, church, or party,*

21. **Envyings,** *which is pain, ill-will, and jealousy at the good fortune or blessing of another,* **murders,** *which is to premeditatively kill a person, or to spoil or mar the happiness of another,* **drunkenness,** *which is a life style of living intoxicated, participation in drinking bouts, and, in truth, being a slave to drink,* **reveling,** *which is lascivious and boisterous feastings and carousing, with obscene music, and other sinful activities,* **and such like. Of the which I tell you before,** *even* **as I have also told** *you* **in time past, that they which** *involve themselves and* **do such things** *as these,* **shall not inherit the Kingdom of God.**

22. **But** *various facet aspects of* **the fruit of the** *Born-Again, recreated, Human* **spirit is love,** *which is divine, and includes strong, tender, compassionate devotion to the wellbeing of another,* **joy,** *which is the emotional delight, gladness, and excitement over blessing expected or received for one's self and for others,* **peace,** *which is the state of quietness, harmony, repose, order, and security in the midst of turmoil, strife, and temptations,* **longsuffering,** *which is patient endurance, able to bear long with the frailties, offenses, injuries, and provocations of others,* *without murmurings, repining, or resentment,* **gentleness,** *which is a disposition to be gentle, soft-spoken, kind, even-tempered, cultured, and refined in character and conduct,* **goodness,** *which is the state of being good and kind, virtuous, benevolent, generous, and God-like in one's life and conduct,* **faith,** *which is the living, divinely implanted, acquired, and created principal of inward and wholehearted confidence, assurance, trust, and reliance on God and all that he says,*

23.   **Meekness,** *which is the disposition to be gentle, kind, indulgent, and even balanced in tempers and passions, and being patient in suffering injuries without feeling a spirit of revenge,* **temperance,** *which is self-control and a moderation in the indulgence of any appetites and passions.* And **against such** *virtues as these* **there is no law.**

24.   **And they that are Christ's,** *and belong to him,* **have** *legally* **crucified the flesh with** *all of* **the affections and lusts** *thereof.*

25.   **If we** *choose to* **live in the** *newly, Born-Again, recreated, Human* **spirit,** *then* **let us also walk,** *in a practical manner, from day to day* **in the** *newly, Born-Again, recreated, Human* **spirit.**

26.   **Let us not be** *unwisely* **desirous of vain glory,** *where we are continually* **provoking one another,** *and* **envying one another.**

CHAPTER 6

1.   Brethren, if a man *stumble, and* be overtaken in a fault, ye which *proclaim that ye* are spiritual, restore such an one in the spirit of meekness;considering thyself, lest thou also *should* be tempted *and fall.*

2.   *When ye are able,* bear ye one another's burdens, and so fulfil the "*Royal* Law" of Christ, *to love your neighbor.*

3.   For if a man think*eth* himself to be something *or somebody,* when he is *really* nothing, he *truly* deceiveth himself.

4.   But let every man *be careful* to prove his own work, and then, *when the time comes,* shall he have rejoicing in himself alone, and not in another.

5.   For every man *ultimately* shall bear his own burden.

6.   Let him that is *well* taught in the word *of God,* communicate unto him that teacheth *others,* in all good things.

7.   Be not deceived; God is not *going to be* mocked: for whatsoevera man *chooseth to* soweth, that shall he also reap.

8.   For he that *chooseth to* soweth to his flesh *or to his soul,* shall of the flesh reap corruption.But he that *chooseth to* soweth to the *newly, Born-Again, recreated*

Human spirit shall of the *Holy* Spirit *of God* reap life everlasting.

9.   And let us not be weary *and faint* in well doing; for in *the* due season we shall reap, if we faint not.

10.   As we have therefore *an* opportunity, let us do good unto all *men*, especially unto them who are of the household of faith.

11.   Ye see how large a letter I have written unto you, *and to the Hebrews at Jerusalem,* with mine own hand.

12.   As many as desire to make *some sort of* a fair shew in the flesh, they *attempt to* constrain you to be circumcised *in accordance with the Law of Moses*; only lest they should *come to the recognition of the truth, and should* suffer persecution *themselves* for the cross of Christ.

13.   For neither *do* they themselves, who are circumcised *in accordance with Moses' commands* keep the law; but *they* desire to have you circumcised, that they may glory *and celebrate* in *compelling you to yield to the dictates of the Law of Moses, concerning* your flesh.

14.   But God forbid that I should glory *in any thing*, save *for* in the cross of our Lord Jesus Christ; by whom the *entire* world is crucified unto me, and I *am crucified through Christ* unto the world.

15.   For in Christ Jesus neither *Jewish* circumcision availeth any thing, nor uncircumcision, but *rather* a **New Creature.**

16.   And as many as *will* walk according to this rule, *then* peace *be* on them, and mercy, and *particularly* upon the **Israel of God.**

17.   From henceforth let no man trouble me *further.*For I bear in my body the *persecution-suffering* marks of the Lord Jesus.

18.   Brethren, *may* the grace of our Lord Jesus Christ *be* with your spirit.Amen.

Meet the Author

By-The-Book Ministries, Inc. began in 2001 as a teaching outreach. Rob E. Daley has been gifted by God to be able to explain biblical truths in an easy to understand manner.

Many have been blessed by his teaching style.

Rob was saved and filled with the Holy Spirit in 1978 and has been instructed by the greatest teacher of all—the Spirit of Truth Himself. Rob is an ordained minister with the Assemblies of God International Fellowship and has pastored in various churches over the past 34 years.

It is the desire of this ministry to see the body of Christ solidly taught, and grow up into the things of the Lord. Rob is available for seminars, retreats, conventions, etc.

Rob can be reached at:

thedaleys@bythebookministries.org

http://robdaleyauthor.com

www.ingramcontent.com/pod-product-compliance
Lightning Source LLC
Chambersburg PA
CBHW020954030426
42339CB00004B/91